In Truth

Other Books by Emanuel di Pasquale

Genesis (Boa, 1980)
The Silver Lake Love Poems (Bordighera Press)
Escapes the Night (Gradiva Publications)
Cartwheel to the Moon (Cricket Books, 2003)
Europa (Gradiva Publications, 2006)
Writing Anew: New and Selected Poems (Bordighera Press, 2007)
Siciliana (Bordighera Press, 2010)
Harvest (Bordighera Press, 2011)
Out of Stars and Sand (Gradiva Publications, 2012)
Love Lines (Bordighera Press, 2013)
The Ocean's Will (Guernica, 2013)
Self-Portrait (NYQ Books, 2014)
Knowing the Moment (Blast Press, 2014)
Poems in Sicily and America (Blast Press, 2016)

In Truth

Emanuel di Pasquale

NY̶Q Books™

The New York Quarterly Foundation, Inc.
New York, New York

The following poems appeared previously in these publications:
Asbury Park Press: "Hawks at Pre-Dawn in New Jersey"
Paterson Literary Review: "Dark in the Sun"

NYQ Books™ is an imprint of The New York Quarterly Foundation, Inc.

The New York Quarterly Foundation, Inc.
P. O. Box 2015
Old Chelsea Station
New York, NY 10113

www.nyq.org

First Edition

Set in New Baskerville

Layout by Raymond P. Hammond

Cover Design by Raymond P. Hammond

Cover Art: *North Shore,* acrylic on canvas, 48 x 36 in. by Steve Northeast | www.stevenortheast.com

Library of Congress Control Number: 2017930515

ISBN: 978-1-63045-040-3

In Truth

Contents

In Truth

*for Raymond Hammond
with appreciation for carrying on the work
of William Packard*

Hawks at Pre-Dawn in New Jersey

Nine hawks dance over the Northern Parkway strip
just off exit 105.
Lit by the two crooked
candles of the waning half-moon
and the sun mounting over the ocean,
they glide, soft as owls,
certain as top ten ice dancers
cavorting on a rink in Manasquan.

Heaven

Last day of June. Slim,
lazy gods, deer doe and fawns,
a family of four,
cross the northwest corner
for my house. Clouds release
the sun. Trees let through a modest breeze.
My wine is half full.
Am I in heaven?

Small Heaven

The lilac and the daffodil
grow like small heavens.
Deer trot in my woods,
and squirrels nestle in my pines.
Dawn sings in light
in the flight of sparrows
and in the symphony of starlings
and turtledoves.

Grey Drizzle

The birds are silent.
Bucks huddle by tree roots.
My head hurts.
Bushes and roses lean down,
droop.
Pine trees rock back and forth,
back and forth.
The hawk, only the hawk,
plays—it flies up and down;
it circles;
it opens the closed air.

The Wren That Forgot to Sing

The wren that forgot to sing
stood tight-throated
in the small opening
of a twilight-green forest
its neck stretched out
its eyes so wide—
attentive to all sounds
behind its head—
sensing hiss of snake,
wing beat of bat.

For LL

To fall on you—as a man,
drunk from love and red wine,
falls on a wheat field!

To gather you—as a man,
for love, gathers flowers:
red and white roses,
blue iris,
purple
violets
and peonies.

The River

I.

I swam under the old bridge,
in the river that joined one hill
of the city to the other
(pigeons hightailing
stretching and shooting out
like fireworks)
a rough stream
breakers, waters blue green white
sharp eddies
snake shoulders
snake heads.
Then at that point
where the river opened widest
deepest
and blue calm
I became lost in the curve of dive
in the spin
my head saying yes yes
my legs dancing

II.

Sat by the shore after
a short rest among the pines
and fig trees.
And the river,
now torrent
ridden by
three small dark horses,
chestnut,
spoke to me:
"These horses need new riders."

Upstream struggled
the small horses—
nostrils wide,
manes thick, black and red,
working at the swim—
their eyes were wide, calm;
no neighing ripped from their throats.
I rose, naked,
by the steep shore…and thought.

The Clown

Looking like wormwood,
the clown lay
on the splinters
of an alabaster bird
and from his youth
sang for death.
The moon, chopped head,
rolls with crooked eyes,
faking a look of love.
The stars beat like fists of fire.
Deep in furnace light,
I am at the farthest dawn,
alone, a roaming thing
in a burning desert.
The palest ghosts wink at me
and, with the points of rusty scissors,
prick the insides of my thighs.
Dry land fences off the seas.
Sand multiplies.
And desert lizards,
their scaly tongues flicking,
are on the loose; their eyes
freeze one or two final birds,
while the hidden webs of spiders
pin the last butterflies.
Death fell on him
like a long face.

Ragusa, Sicily

Always the children rushing like small sparrows,
their little bruises needing care
from older sisters or grandmothers.
Play never stopped with their quick tears—
bread munched in the breakaway at tag,
a hurried drink at the public fountain before hide and seek,
or while players were being chosen for a soccer game.
And always the church bells like comforting songs—
night and day, night and day,
louder and sharper on the holidays,
or on the day of the dead when widows,
rosaries wrapped around their wrists like chains,
wailed like witches.

The Hero

Forget the evergreen, slow creeper,
stiffening its nail-like leaves.
Forget the hothouse warriors:
tender tulip, gladiola,
the bachelor cyclamen...

The hero is the elm, the oak,
the dogwood, the apple tree
in deep freeze—its lovers
the wind, frost, and ice.

The Rage-Filled Day

These marble wings hovering
over the boy's grave are the boy
as he died in the season of mud
when, curious for tadpoles and small snakes,
he stepped barefoot
in the sleeping whirlpool
of a muddy puddle,
and, feeling wings in his hands,
shaped tongues of birds from clay.
Oh, how he joyed in the screech of swallow,
in the early walnut moon,
in the moist caverns god
had punched on a rage-filled day.
And in such a cavern,
from whose entrance blossomed
lime and almond trees,
he settled
and drank mountain waters
and echoed the silver singing of the cormorant
and forgot night and forgot day
even as the sun,
like a sailboat on fire,
curlicue ships,
sailed the skies.

A Memory

Am I that young man by the sea?
Knee bent
leaning a bit to the side
inviting someone to join in
as the waves huff and roll.
Am I that young man by the sea?
Hair mimics the brown algae
loose in the Maine winds.

Did I call for the dolphin?
Did I call for the salt and sea?

The Virgin's Curse

While the moon loiters
in the late afternoon,
wearing a spotted,
see-through camisole,
the blinding sun flares
curlicues,
chartering red-tongued passageways,
but the moon,
pale girl,
wastes the night
lolling in the skies—
well out of the way
of the dragon-throated sun

.

When the End Comes

When the end comes,
a red rain,
a quake that cracks schools and churches,
a brown ash that wafts
like mangled birds,
we walk to the waters
to become one with the dolphin and the whale.

We hold the little ones in our arms
in the hope that love
can make shield of bone.

In the high winds
the gulls sing their siren songs.

And we sleep knowing
that through night
struggles the advent of day.

There rises sun in morning,
rises like the eye in the palm of the hand
of a disjoined god—but rises.

A Greater Love

Orpheus is the music in our bones
the reverberations from the oceanic depths
of after love
when the brain and body find peace
in the undercurrents of waters
lapping silently in moonless midnights

Orpheus is the ripple of a child's belly
in open laughter

Orpheus is the wind twanging phone lines
voyaging dogwood autumn leaf

Orpheus is the raindrop on your nipple
lingering lingering to the pull of suck
licking it with the love of gravity
tracing tracing it
sculpting it as it falls

Mid-November Night

Save for the dumb, intermittent light
of a jet, or the blind light up on some tower,
the sky, cobwebbed by low grey clouds
and black heights, is dark tonight.
Both the moon and Venus,
and all stars, distant
and near, seem to have shut their eyes.
It is the blackest night.
Lost in my smallness,
I shoot out my own inner light
and search the skies,
hoping the blue galactic brooch
or Venus will shine
like triangular diamonds.

Thoughts

It can't be.
Her heart can't be closed.
I see it open, winged,
leap out of her eyes.
I see the sweet shiver
on her face; I see it
descend
through her limbs
like the free wave
on high water.
It can't be.
Her heart can't be closed.
I hear it in her voice,
its joy singing
from her bones,
cells,
the chambers
of her very heart.

An Etruscan in New Jersey

A squirrel is a statue
on a December oak branch;
its tail asks a question.
And in my mind
stream browning meadows,
fields of poppies—
a red
ocean
in flight
turned
blue
in the
upper
heights.

The Dead Speak

Bones now frozen
in this clay
were supple once
with marrow;
blood leaped from brain
to fingertips.

We looked at stars
and knew a presence
in their fire,
felt it settling
in our core.

We fought with lovers
for a sigh.

Hearing loss
in the moan of church bells,
we rushed to hug our children.
The lilac and the daffodil
grew for us
like small heavens;
leaves fell,
eager to enact a story.

Deer traced our woods,
and squirrels nestled in our pines.

Dawn sang to us
in colors and in light,
sang to us easily
in the flight of sparrows
and in the symphony
of turtledoves
and starlings.

Should I Die

Bury me in wet sand
by the sea

Let my bones
in the flesh-eating tomb
reverberate
to the hoarse, whispering waters

Let the spinning
half-circling winds
fade
in the fingers
of the sun

And let the
moonlight
pinpoint
silver lizards
swimming
through the iris shore

Remembrance

A sea of gulls
above the sea
like spotted nets
or chunks of clouds fallen
or wave crests risen
and the Atlantic never still

Dive as deep as sea floor
seep past sea floor
into the bion-burning dirt
and molten earth
and the stone never still
and the sky never still
and my heart never still

Remembrance of Sicily (Ragusa)

I.

You lie stretched on a hill
churches encircle you like vines
water fountains
palm trees dripping honey
August asphalt melting
into silver sticking streams
children and pigeons humming
in church gardens
children and swallows
outrunning the cool
sun at twilight
old men bent like crushed snakes
on cement benches
and the sweet stars
pitching silver filaments
over the heads of lovers
in the mulberry fields

II.

Old women locked in single rooms they
call houses
stay surrounded by ten-foot
thick walls of stone

Where streams ran wild
at every rut
in a long yesterday
the waterfalls are now drying
the sky holds back the rain that sweetens
orange and almond grove

III.

Fossilized bird tongues
trapped inside rocks
buried under dry rivers
hold rain songs
but the moon that once caught
their trills and incense dreams
remembers

Do you remember me my Sicily
do you recall a child
wide-eyed little beast
beating about your wheat and poppy fields?

Old Sicilian Woman's Last Prayer

No god spurred by imagined or real wrongs
or cackled at by a goddess jealous
of the old woman's wisdom
plotted against her that day.
(Her in-house gods, the old Roman
masters that had yessed her seed
were sleeping the stone's sleep.)
No thunder, no lightning was shaped
to slay her; it was her will
that stilled her,
for after eighty years
even the occasional joy
had become a burden:
sweet figs were hard to find
even in season,
the black grape
seemed all pits,
and all around people
had grown silent;
only the cool marble of churches spoke to her.
"Bury me in a river," she wrote
on the back of her father's photograph.
And added, "Find one, quickly,
for we live in a land
where all the rivers are drying."

Filaments

This page that spells out
words of simple love to you—
I want
to fly
for you,
with you—
will crumble fall
like storm-torn butterfly
or color-drunk leaf
caught in the No
of time,
just as my heart
falls crumbles
from your
No!
Yet
lovers tomorrow
who will silently
etch their grief
in burning hieroglyphics
shall build
new monuments of blood
and fill new pages.

Invocation

You walk in with Venus at its highest,
and from your hands waft hints of the sun.
Yes, you come to me in silence,
and your eyes say, "Swim in my lake,
my beloved." And easily
a small wind becomes visible
in the lifting of the yellow satin drapes
and of your red night gown.
Your small shoulders lean to me,
and I catch you in my arms
as a loving forest hermit catches
a turtledove to sing with it
for an instant
and then to let her free—
so that she may find joy
in her fierce flight
and on a day return to him.
All is whispering
and a dancing of spinning lights,
a tintinnabulation
and a remembrance of galactic swirls.
It is all bright.
My lips kiss
your lips
and softly suck
your breasts
and then our bodies,
one in love,
become a lake
stirred by an overwhelming
undercurrent from the sea
that gently retreats
and slows the wild waves
to a ripple and a heartbeat—
and then I kiss your eyes.

Many Times During the Day

Many times during the day—
when I read ancient poetry,
the unwritten word,
the word meant to be sung,
I pause and think of you.
You are not made of peonies,
although the same life force made you,
but your flesh has the crispness,
the consistency of peonies;
and like the peony,
the healing flower
named in honor of the
physician of the gods,
Apollo himself,
you heal—
your hands warm and firm
that can stir dull stillness
into movement, flow;
your eyes that in their openness
unlock mine into brightness,
your eyes that in their softness
loosen the silvery wing tips
of my blood.
Many times during the day—
when I look at my daughter
as she seriously studies
or as she smilingly
longs for her young man,
I think of you—
and then all the birds
in all the fields
sing.

Thoughts

What is it with the sea and sky?
The stars, silver dolphins,
swim in wide arches
as the earth,
a small blue whale,
turns belly up,
bent on drowning, delighted,
chasing its own tail.
And the sea,
spill free, hushed and cupped
by God's weighty hand,
foams, leaps like
a fluid sun.
And always the greater ocean,
where both sea and sky swim
like beads of light
in the blue day,
in the black night.

A Mid-March Love Poem

Three days into March, I heard
my first dawn bird,
and trees and grass—
that had kept the faith
through a winter of ice
that cracked willow and starfish—
took a deep breath
and easily shook loose their
tightness.

And now the forsythia
resettles its yellow hair,

the hyacinth rises
on green tongues,

the oak branch swells
with rust-colored pearls,

and two redbreasts that sing
even in the noonday
are building a nest
on the lowest branch
of a blue fir.

Thoughts for Her at Year's End

(Bright is the world
sped on by light)

In cold December's end,
I think of you
knowing we live
in the same azure house
and sense your silver breath
in the night sky,
where new stars are born
over and over
like lovers
in sexual embrace

Fireflies and Light

I.

The singing of fireflies
is like the rush of love
when bones hum
like the waters
of high seas.

II.

Light has no color;
it gives color:
blue to fir,
green to lizards.
It is all black in darkness,
where even the blue-engorged bion
sleeps.

III.

The eye can see no farther
than the stars,
and I see as far as you.

I Was Buried When My Father Died

I was buried
when my father died

My pallet
his wife's widowed
bed

Outside among the eyes of day
the river fed wild dog dove
iris radish lemon grove…

For lack of peonies and
chrysanthemums
there was the stink
of unwashed flesh, sweat
heft of breath

Outside among the eyes of day
the river fed wild dog dove
iris radish lemon grove…

While my father's body melted
to his sweet and lean bones
in the wild aloneness
of flesh-eating grave
I lay in the slush
of wet kisses
even as my eyes
glanced away from
the icy nipples and
overripe thighs
of my mother
as she cooled
my genitals

in the folds of
her grey tunic

Outside among the eyes of day
the river fed wild dog dove
iris radish lemon grove...

Steady

There is no shifting of this love to another.
It is for you,
who hold so many kisses
yet give so few,
for you, who hold so many embraces
yet cross them over your heart.

The northern lights,
woven scarves of sun stuff,
dance like golden and blue snakes
to the song of solar winds.
Oh, love, dance to my song,
naked chords of love for you.

On Valentine's Day

On Valentine's Day,
I go out in my backyard,
and, in birds' tongues,
speak to sparrows, cardinals and robins
and thank them for their feathers
and their songs.

And in the happy chatter
of the slim and lovely dolphin,
I dive into the ocean
and sing songs of ease,
songs of peace.

To a Schizophrenic

Your brain will not sift chaff from grain,
rake pale weed into garbage heaps
and hoard the good sun blood.
To you, each bit, gold or crap,
lights up the universal black.

An End

No sandpiper has visited.
Summer rolls down the hill,
a stone loosened by rain and dampness
and the hiss of time.
This early Saturday in August,
the sun comes up at two-thirty
and the ocean stinks
dragging brown puke on its back.
The seagulls do not sing,
silent at the edge of water.
A rust and silver pigeon
moves heavy-footed.
Drowned feathers, burned wood
smash against rocks.
(And you elsewhere.)

Giovanni Iacono

I.

His voice had wings
as when at dawn
small sails are raised
from the bellies of boats
and stretched open for the new sky.

II.

You could smell pine trees in him,
river water, lemon rind, the sea.
And in his eyes, burning in brown,
you could see the fire of earth
lifting cedar, cornstalk, chestnut.

III.

All sea-glass was jewelry to him,
green bits of emerald,
white shards of diamonds—
slivers of iodine bottles
transfigured into burning garnet.

IV.

And in long summer days,
down the Irminio river,
he knew which rocks
covered soft-shelled crabs
and which covered
spring water rivulets.
Watermelons he buried
in river shallows sang red,
and corncob he roasted
turned hickory and honey.

Seven Seagulls

I wait for you this mid-November dawn
as you drive from Virginia to New Jersey,
from your mares, wide-hipped,
from your barn, red,
from your pond and its frog chorus,
scabrous lyrics,
to where seven seagulls row
south over an ocean of gold slivers.
Your silver earrings,
wind-turned olive leaves,
huddle at the feet
of the small statue of Venus,
whose shadow stretches from the windowsill
over my bed. I wait by the breaking waves,
envious of their steady heartbeat.
(Your hair a handle and your arching head
throat opening lips shaping into the circle of love)

For Sharon

When Sharon talks, hummingbird wings flutter
her song is the breath of daffodils
her eyes illuminate
like the greater light
and when she sings
the entire earth rocks and rolls
her red toenails are early
sunrise and sunsets
and when she walks
the winds and deer
learn from her grace.

Ruth

She runs like truth
clear
as natural as doe
or dawn
like water
fluid as April
hushed rain in gentle
western wind
no rush
a steady flow
her eyes
her smile
aglow

In Praise of Long Branch

In Long Branch
the boardwalk rise,
a rainbow of salt spray
and spinning waves
of seagull flight
and plaintive sandpiper quick run.
Praise the rebirth
in word, in laughter, and in song.

The Bob Dylan Incident

When Bob Dylan walked into Morris Avenue and shifted
south on Joline, looking for something (remembrances
of Bruce?), dressed in rain rubber boots and two pairs of
sweatpants, he wandered here and there, until he found
himself in a well-kept yard.

The lady of the house called the city cops who questioned
this strange person, trouble lady as they thought.

"I am Bob Dylan," said Bob.

"You don't look like Bob Dylan," said the lady cop and
called her sergeant.

Who also said, "You don't look like Bob Dylan."

So they took him to Ocean Place Hotel where Willie Nelson
and John Mellencamp bailed him out.

"Yes, he is for sure Bob Dylan," they all said.

And so Bob Dylan lost in Long Branch
eventually said, "What do they know in Long Branch, a city
lost by the sea?"

And as the bus pulled away from Ocean Place, the cops
waved and smiled as Bob Dylan was driven away.

For Dempster Leech, Thespian

Acclaimed as the new Orson Wells,
Sweet bells rang
When Dempster acted under Mrs. Kelly,
She of the goat teeth
And liquid eyes. What prizes his voice won:
Long Island this…Long Island that…
And so he rode the train to the Village
To try serious Off Broadway.
But it didn't pan out…no gold in dry gulch.
Adventurous, big-eyed slayer,
He took to private detecting in Chinatown.
Another arroyo. They found him hanging
From a bathroom stall at the Schubert,
Dangling like a puppet.

On the Resurgence of Long Branch's Boardwalk

Women, men, hardhats, using their hands, their sturdy shoulders,
Riding machines like gods—
Unearthed broken rocks, cracked wood of ancient pylons—
Settled the earth down with powerful dirt, cement with the steadying
Force of lava, supreme rocks, volcanic driven...
And now the boardwalk knows its strength...
Steel, tungsten, hardy wood fused with unguents mercurial—
The light poles begin to rise, warriors bringing the good flame, light.
Bushes spread out on sand at the edge of street,
And all is ready for our city's rebirth.

Dark in the Sun

I.

She swears by astral revelations.
"Our minds knew each other before
our bodies met," and is certain
that the great fire at Alexandria
did not burn a thing.
"All the knowledge in those books
stayed in the minds
of those who knew,
and was passed on,
and is." She is sure,
although at the word fire
she grows chill
and will not hear of sun
and energy today.
"You have frightened me," she says.
"No more talk of fire, please."

II.

"I only know I talk with
my other self long after
our conversation's done,"
she whispers.
"I find poems I don't remember writing,"
she shouts and reads, "Streams…prayers…tears."

"Still, you can find these poems
in you, and you can recall
these conversations with this
other self," I encourage her.

"It frightens me. How can these
two selves merge into one? Highways

melt when I drive. Solid lines
divide. But you can't possibly
know. You can't know my fear."
"I am listening and
don't presume to know.
But you sound so clear-headed now,
and the merging is beginning
to happen."

"Don't laugh at me,"
she warns helplessly.
"There is no laughter here."

The Seeming Dead Orchid Blossoms

for Richard Wilbur

Like the light skin of a graceful aged Lady
the last two flowers, pink and white, fell over the black earth
of the burgundy vase, only two thick green leaves alive.
Over three months all was still.
Until two small tendrils peeped
at opposite sides…small, small
and then began to slightly curl
unfurl and then stirred into white
bud and overnight ramified
into pink flower.

Garden State Parkway

Soft snow swirls
along the parkway:
Albino butterflies.

Agamemnon, Notes from Hades

The embarrassment wasn't in the death,
not the red carpet, the net, not being slaughtered
by that bitch and that boyfriend of hers. (What's his name?)
After all, lions fall to weak hunters.
The little things haunt me: she drooled in her anger;
crossed her eyes in the love bed;
sucked my nipples as if I were her mother.
The guy's face was girlish.
Listen, those two children of mine getting caught in the myth
was worth my having died.

Long Branch Watchtower

On Assumption day, I swam in the high tide waters
while my wife and daughter
sat on the lifeguard towers.
My child made sand angels,
and my wife led us in a dance of ring around
the land, a pocketful of sand.
The waters were clear as my child was fair.
The waters were near
as my wife was true.
And the waves would not
stand still.

In Belmar, We Bury Birds in the Ocean

Did the blue-green swallow
see its image as it rushed at breakneck speed
into the glass wall,
or packed in its own energy
was it lost in joy of movement, flight?
No matter, although for a while it held its living heat,
at impact it was no longer bird;
it had lost its song
and its flight had ended even in memory.
Why let this child of sun and air
rot in a crack on earth?
In Belmar, we bury birds in the ocean-
for one last flight and food for blue fish and crab.

Dove

I had a love.
She went away.
Wounded dove.
What's more to say?

Li-Po

The emperor, wrapped in sexual embrace,
has soldiers drag me to the royal bed.
While naked girls hold up a blue silk screen,
I describe the sweat on the lady's nipples,
beads of jade.
Pleased, the emperor orders eunuchs to their knees,
and has them pull off my boots.
My poems swell, grape in autumn vineyard.
As the moon rolls like a loose barrel,
I sit by a green lake.
The mountain winds cool my bare head.
I sing and drink wine all night long.

Michelangelo

When asked why his angels
were as sperm-eyed as far-tailed Minos,
Michelangelo said, "I have known the natural violence of flowers
and know the brazen serpent is too long to be constrained."

Snow-Clearing

A Boston Parks Commissioner has five feet of snow
piled up on the city's graveyards.

The bones of Winthrop, Wilson, Mather, Chillingdale,
frozen ever as they lived, shiver into sharpness.
The tombstones, scabrous tongues,
welcome the fingers of God pressing cold, twisting.
The salt-rough slabs embrace the snow
as rocks into filthy waters embrace moss.

Man Dies Hunting Trinkets in Sewer
in New York City

Outside Yankee Stadium, at River Avenue,
descended the three friends, Nunez, Alvarado and Cancel,
searching for silver dollars, bracelets and rings.
Packing flashlight descended the three friends,
searching for gold teeth burning in the silt and rising waters.
In the South Bronx, Alvarado descended with memories
of the $135 he had once found. Bound in their dream,
they descended, having hung a plastic bag
on the rungs as point of reference.
Frightened in the pitch-black darkness, unsteady
in the rising waters, Nunez fell. dead in the treasure hunt,
lost in the currents. Shattered in the skull,
Nunez fell. A cracked hull...

For Elisabeth, My Daughter

After a thirteen hour sleep, you rise like Trinacria,
your two feet bent at the ankles, your hands clasped over your
    forehead,
my Sicily. "I'm Sleeping Beauty," you laugh.
Your eyes, brown with a touch of green, burn with Emerald fire.
    My Ireland.
For you, the two islands (lost at sea; open on all points) merge:
You weep when you hear children cry,
your toys are fruits to share;
for you, trees fly, lamps are umbrellas, and hand wild birds.
My daughter, you glide from room to room
and swim in the narrow streams of the hallway
while outside the ocean sings to you with unfurling breakers
and with spinning winds.

Father and Son

My son calls. "Pop, drive over. I'm in a hole
five feet deep,
a foot short of legal burial.
I've been digging for the main water pipe,
found it, and cracked it with the pick—poor workmanship,
the town water people tell me.
Someone covered the pipe with cement.
I had no way to tell I was hitting pipe."
I drive over to my ex-wife's house, my old house,
and find my son ready—tar and waterproof tape near the 'grave.'
"Only an Indian could be buried here, Paul, sitting.
You'd have to break his spear in two to fit him regally."
He wants me to walk into the house. I want to
decline, but walk in and feel the heft.
I walk out feeling three hundred years old.
Powerful mint I once planted in the yard stands thick.

Our Unsteady World

The earth moves too fast
it spins and spins
without its steady flow
pine trees fly off into the skies
the oceans broil inward
and wild winds
shut song of joy
and truth
rain overwhelms
bushes and grass
a disarray
what silver candle will not be blow away?
what child's cry will survive?

The New York Quarterly Foundation, Inc.
New York, New York

Poetry
Magazine

Since 1969

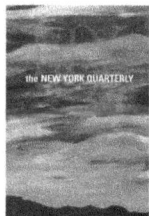

Edgy, fresh, groundbreaking, eclectic—voices from all walks of life.

Definitely NOT your mama's poetry magazine!

The *New York Quarterly* has been defining the term contemporary American poetry since its first craft interview with W. H. Auden.

Interviews • Essays • and of course, lots of poems.

www.nyq.org

No contest! That's correct, NYQ Books are NO CONTEST to other small presses because we do not support ourselves through contests. Our books are carefully selected by invitation only, so you know that NYQ Books are produced with the same editorial integrity as the magazine that has brought you the most eclectic contemporary American poetry since 1969.

Books

www.nyq.org

www.ingramcontent.com/pod-product-compliance
Lightning Source LLC
LaVergne TN
LVHW091231080426
835509LV00009B/1241